Don't Forget to Download Your Two Bonus Gifts!

Because you bought this shook, you get two valuable, *must-have* bonus gifts I created exclusively for readers of Main Street Author.

The first gift is a "lost chapter" on *The Power of Undivided Attention*, which I wrote after finalizing Main Street Author but want you to have.

The second gift is a special companion training, *How to Design & Print Your Shook,* I created just for readers of *Main Street Author.* This exclusive training, which complements this shook, goes into greater detail on how to design your cover and interior and how to print your shook. It gives you *must-have* insights you should know to get your shook done quickly and easily!

DOWNLOAD TODAY!

www.MainStreetAuthor.com/gifts

ALSO BY MIKE CAPUZZI

Dream, Inc.

The Ultimate Success Secret (with Dan Kennedy)

3 Steps to Incredible Response

The Entrepreneur's Guide to Marketing with PURLs

High Impact Marketing Manifesto

Masters of the Mastermind

Just Do This

The Magic of Short Books

WIN WIN WIN

**The Ultimate Guide for Main Street
Business Owners to Author, Publish and
Profit From a Short, Helpful Book**

MIKE CAPUZZI

5 STAR PRAISE FOR
MAIN STREET AUTHOR

"Mike Capuzzi hits the nail square with his latest book, *Main Street Author*. As a multi-book author myself, I've seen the power books hold in the marketplace. They anoint celebrity, exclusivity and authority like no other media available to entrepreneurs. Mike's book breaks this all down into bite-sized steps that anyone can follow. If you're wondering how you can stand out in your marketplace, in your profession—no matter if you're a dentist, physician, attorney, CPA, roofing contractor or whatever, a well-written, professionally designed book following Mike's formula will lift you well past any competition and MAKE YOU the choice of your avatar clients, patients or customers. Get his book NOW. And, read it."

Jerry A. Jones
CEO of Jerry Jones Direct

"Just finished this very powerful little book. Only took me an hour to read it, but it is packed with valuable information for any businessperson who understands the importance of being an author. Capuzzi breaks the process down to an understandable system."

Frank Lombardo
Independent Pharmacist

"After reading *Main Street Author*, I now have a clear path to success for writing a book (I actually have four books in mind!). For the first time since I had the idea to write a book years ago, I'm truly excited about the process, which is a lot nicer than feeling overwhelmed. Thank you Mike for helping a small business owner like me become an author!"

Ben Turshen
Founder of Ben Turshen Meditation

"Mike Capuzzi has given a simple yet powerful complete marketing tool. The book was a lesson and an example of what to do. I usually purchase Kindle books when I have a choice because they are easier on my old eyes. But once I completed this one, I knew I needed to order the physical book too so I could experience the "shook" principle in my own hands. In the age of high tech 'hacks,' this was a straightforward marketing principle any business could use to stand out."

Dr. Ginger Bratzel
Founder of New Patient Attraction Automation

"Having written and published a book the old-fashioned and time-consuming way, I find Mike's step-by-step formula for getting a book done just brilliant. I agree 100% with Mike that having a short, focused book that gets read is far more useful and impressive than having a longer book that no one will ever read."

Bernie Heer
Employee Benefits Advisor

PUBLISHED BY BITE SIZED BOOKS
A DIVISION OF PERSISTENT MARKETING, INC.

Copyright © 2019 by Mike Capuzzi

Print ISBN: 978-1-7325127-6-4
Ebook ISBN: 978-1-7325127-9-5

112219

Bite Sized Books publishes short, helpful books or shooks™ for Main Street business owners to attract new customers. Shooks are easy-to-create, quick-to-read short books. They are designed to be read by prospective customers, clients or patients, in about an hour. Bite Sized Books offers a painless process to enable entrepreneurs and business owners to benefit from the authority that comes from being a published author, without the hassle and time commitment normally associated with writing a book. Do you have an idea for a bite sized book you would like us to publish? Visit BiteSizedBooks.com for more details.

CONTENTS

"It never occurred to me that I could write a book nor that I had material that would appeal to our dentist target clients. Thankfully, I first listened to Mike Capuzzi's teaching on the subject of short books and then made the decision to work with him to create one. My co-author and I are glad we did. Mike guided us (and prodded us) during the entire process. Working with him to create the plan, content and final book was easy and fast.

"I highly recommend any serious business owner who wants to get a client-attraction book done to work with Mike."

—Doug Brown, co-author of
Becoming Your Patients' Hero

WHO SHOULD READ
THIS BOOK?

E ven though this is a short book, designed to be read in about an hour, I don't want to waste your time if it's not a good fit. Take a few minutes and read this entire section to see if *Main Street Author* is a smart investment of your time and energy.

First and foremost, *Main Street Author* is **NOT** for the person who is looking to make money by selling his or her book, nor is it for the person who is looking for worldwide fame and recognition. There are many *how-to* books and book publishing services for people looking for widespread fame.

Instead, my focus is on helping the local business owner become the recognized expert and authority in his or her local community by becoming a book author and leveraging a book-centric marketing strategy. Specifically, I wrote *Main Street Author* for two types of business owners:

1. The local Main Street business owner who has a place of business where people visit in order to buy the products or services. These types of business owners are professional service providers, including lawyers, insurance agents, financial advisors; healthcare professionals, including dentists, physicians, chiropractors, therapists; and high-ticket or luxury product/service providers, including certain types of retailers, real estate professionals.

2. The business owner who serves local Main Street businesses, including tax professionals, business and marketing services, technology service providers, software developers, etc.

If you fall into one of the above categories, you will be happy to know I wrote this book just for you and your specific needs, requirements and opportunities. After working with thousands of Main Street business owners over the past two decades, I get these types of businesses and what it takes to survive and thrive in the 21st century, which is why I decided to write *Main Street Author*—specifically for these three primary reasons:

1. To share a unique type of _short, helpful book_ (the shook™) I believe Main Street business owners should leverage in their business and give you a step-by-step formula to create one.

2. To shift your focus from traditional, *everybody has one* marketing tools like brochures, to an authority-building, customer-attraction asset—your own shook.

3. To invite readers to connect with me so we can determine if working together to publish a shook is the right next step.

I am a *"what you see is what you get"* kind of guy, and I'm not shying away from the fact that while my intention is to open your eyes to a new marketing asset for your business, I also want readers who get what I have to offer, to "raise their hand" and reach out to me to see if working together makes sense.

I am perplexed when people criticize business book authors for "selling too much" in their books because, in my opinion, not enough business-related books offer readers a "next step." This next step should be a helpful continuation of the book's promise and I believe is a critical part of the book.

Today, more than ever before, people are seeking quality information to help them make smart decisions, save time and avoid mistakes. If you and your products/services can do this, why would you be squeamish about letting people know how you can help them and offering a logical next step?

I am unapologetically "selling" in this shook, not only the concept of a shook and why I think it's a superior type of book for you to create but also why working directly with me to publish your short business book is a smart and effective shortcut to success and quick completion.

Finally, *Main Street Author* was written for the person who agrees with these seven beliefs:

1. Time is the most precious gift in our lives, and if we can connect and help others while taking up less, we will be rewarded.

2. The written word containing useful information is one of the best ways to communicate why your products or services will help others solve a problem or take advantage of a new opportunity.

3. Sharing your personal story and stories of how you have helped others will uniquely humanize you and be the beginning of a mutually beneficial relationship between you and your readers.

4. You only have a moment to grab the interest of your targeted prospective customers amid the onslaught of competing marketing messages they are exposed to every day. Once you have their attention with a shook in their hands, you will have a more focused opportunity to communicate why they should invest in your product or service.

5. A real, professionally "constructed" printed book is one of the most powerful advantages and unique game changers in the business world for posi-

tioning you and attracting more ideal customers.

6. Short books are a welcomed relief from *books with bloat*, which contain unnecessary filler and are started but typically never completed by readers.

7. A shook is a worthy business asset for you to create and working with me is the key to getting it done fast and pain-free.

If you are like me and believe you can balance helpful written content with making the case for you and your business, and you are not afraid of making specific, "next step" offers for your readers to take, I wrote this shook for you, so please keep reading.

"I met Mike at a marketing conference and immediately realized he was the guy who could help me get the book I wanted to write finally done. Within three months of meeting Mike, my first shook, *Medicare Made-to-Order* is done and already helping me generate quality prospect leads for my agency. One of the best things about working with Mike were the weekly calls with me, which kept me on track and moving forward. Mike and his shook-publishing service get my highest recommendation!"

—Matthew Petruso, author of
Medicare Made-to-Order

MY PROMISE TO YOU

I t is my sincerest belief that publishing a short, helpful book (shook) is the key to being recognized as a significant, respected and valued expert and it's attainable when you become a Main Street Author. This shook shows you how and I promise to make *Main Street Author* a valuable use of your money, time and attention.

Within the next 60 minutes or so, my intention is to open your eyes to the possibility and value of publishing your own shook and motivate you to take action and get started with your own short book.

I will minimize the hype and bloat (found in a lot of business books), get right to the point and share the essentials of what you need to know to author a shook. Before we move on, I have two reminders for you. Regardless of whether you call the consumers you serve, patients, students, or clients—for simplicity I will refer to them as "customers" throughout the rest of this shook.

Also, you will notice a blatant absence of trying to convince you to write a book for your business. There are a number of books which make the case for why you should have a book. A search on Amazon will reveal many options.

I'm assuming if you are reading these words, you know the transformational power of what having a professionally designed, printed book can do for you and your business.

Your book will be a valuable and long-lasting business asset which you will leverage for years, and there is no denying that being a published author:

- Increases your name (or brand) recognition.
- Enhances your reputation.
- Boosts believability.
- Builds trust.
- Establishes authority.

Being a business owner who is also an author allows you to advertise, market and sell at a higher, more sophisticated level where you attract customers instead of pursuing them.

The is the promise and magic of being a Main Street Author!

INTRODUCTION

I love books. I have a large library, including several rare first edition classics. I have published seven books prior to this one and have helped several business owners publish their own books. To me, there is nothing like a real, <u>printed</u> book, and there is nothing like the feeling of handing somebody your book and watching their expression as they realize you're the author.

But as I stated previously, I am not a book "purist" and don't subscribe to the common way of thinking books should be void of promotion, marketing and selling. I also don't believe books should be filled with unnecessary content simply to reach a specific page count so the publisher can charge a certain amount for the book.

This is why I've developed the shook—a short, helpful book, which follows a specific three-part, Capuzzi-developed formula:

1. Shooks are designed so you can create them quickly and easily. My Main Street Author Programs give you a step-by-step system.

2. Shooks are designed so your targeted reader can read them cover to cover in a single sitting in about an hour or so. I personally don't subscribe to the notion, "It doesn't matter if a person reads your book, you just want to have one." I believe if you have something helpful and important to share, why wouldn't you want them to read your entire book?

3. Shooks have embedded *passive* calls-to-action, which give your readers additional value while enabling you to build a valuable database of prospects. Shooks also include a clear, *active* "next step" for interested readers.

While some may scoff at the concept of a shook, it's been my experience most people **LOVE** them. They don't take much time to read. They help solve a single problem or present a single opportunity, and they offer a chance for readers to continue the relationship with you—the author.

My goal with *Main Street Author* is to open your eyes to the profitable possibilities of what a shook can do for you and your business. If you've never written a book before, a shook is the perfect type of book for you to start with (no novice mountain climber climbs Mt. Everest first), and if you are an experienced author, a shook or series of shooks could be a perfect addition to your existing offering.

The business owner interested in publishing a shook is not concerned with trying to obtain "bestseller status." While there are many people who will try to convince you becoming an "Amazon Best-seller" is important, I believe it's really a misguided distraction for most Main Street Authors. I won't get into all the details of why I believe this, but the reality is that manufactured best-selling status today is commonplace, and if everyone is a best-selling author, then nobody really is. For the most part, I believe the status of being a bestseller has lost its meaning and is nothing more than marketing smoke and mirrors.

Instead, I want you to focus on a problem your target reader has and show him/her how you can fix it, and there is no better way to accomplish this than by being a Main Street Author and creating a shook. Your shook is a sales tool designed to attract more customers. Sure, you might make a few dollars, but don't let this and the manufactured "be a bestseller" distract you from your real goal—attracting more prospects who match your ideal customer profile.

So now that you have a better idea of why I authored this shook and where I stand on some fundamental principles, I urge you to clear your head of any preconceived ideas and beliefs and open your mind to the idea of becoming a Main Street Author.

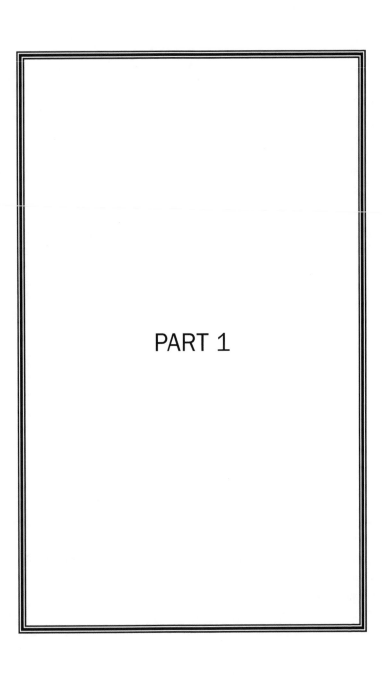

PART 1

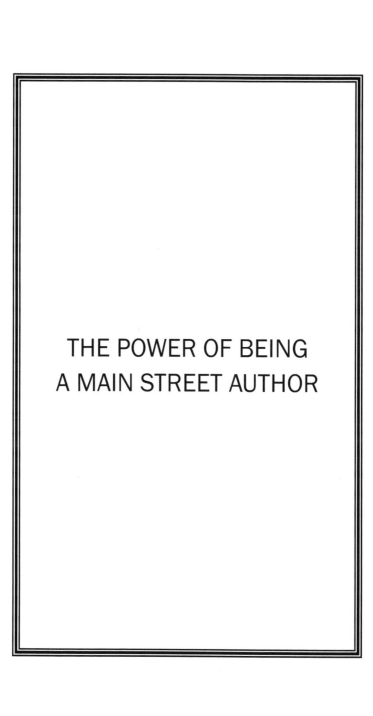

THE POWER OF BEING
A MAIN STREET AUTHOR

"As soon as I heard about Mike's shooks, I knew it was the perfect type of book for me to write as my first book. Mike has made the authoring process simple and fast, and I know my prospective clients appreciate the quick read. I have used my first shook as the primary marketing piece for my 'Dream 100' list of clients and have just finished my second shook on easy meditation tips for business owners."

—Adam Weber, author of
*The Appraisal Review Survival Guide &
From Stress to Profit*

CHAPTER 1

THE CASE FOR SHORT, HELPFUL BOOKS

Books have been an effective way for business owners to offer helpful information to solve a specific problem for over 100 years. In my research, I have found advertisements which have featured a "free book" as far back as 1903, when the Ostermoor Mattress Company offered their book, *The Test of Time*, to individuals interested in getting a better night's sleep.

Throughout the 20th century, books were offered to consumers who have a specific problem or desire, as a tool to help them. It's no different in the 21st century, and after a review of printed ads, television commercials and social media marketing, you still find books being used as a way to help and connect.

A *bite sized* book, focused on a single topic with easy-to-read content, is still one of the most effective "attract new customer" assets you can create. As I mentioned earlier, there are many books already written about the importance of having a book working for you and your business. But there is one big, critical difference today—the lack of free time available for people to read your book and for you to write it.

Most consumers (my guess is 95%) don't have the time or attention span to read long books, regardless of the subject's importance or interest level. They may start with the best of intentions, but after a few chapters, something else gets their attention and the book is put down, never to be completed.

Unfortunately, the promise of the book, the reason they started to read it, is never fulfilled, which is why there is a trend for traditional business books to be getting shorter (not quite shook length, but down to less than 300 pages). How many people have time to read a 300-page book these days?

Recently, I was given a business book as a gift. It's a current book by a big-name Internet marketing expert. As soon as I opened the box and saw it, my first reaction was, "That's a really long book." Coming in at over 400 pages, the book's length resulted in the immediate (and typical) decision to simply lay it aside and maybe get to it at some point in the future.

Contrast this to your perception when you received this shook you are reading now. Did its size intimidate you or invite you to read it? Did you find my promise of a short, quick read appealing?

Think about your own reading habits. When was the last time you actually finished a book (other than the anticipated finishing of this one)? If you're like the business owners I surveyed for this shook, more than 80% of you have not finished a business book you've started within the past year. I get it, and I am in the same boat for a number of reasons.

Yes, there are times you have picked up a book thinking one thing, and then after starting it you realize it's a different thing, but that's not the critical mistake many authors make. I think people make their books unnecessarily long for the wrong reasons, with the main one being they simply don't know how to create bite sized content that is pithy and powerful.

French author Blaise Pascal wrote in 1657, "*I have made this letter longer than usual, only because I have not had the time to make it shorter.*"

Read that quote again, because it's a powerful and important reminder for crafting effective content.

Developing a short, concise and powerful message is no easy task, and it takes more effort to create it than to bloviate and spew everything you know about your product or service. I call it going from "blah, blah, blah to BIG AH-HA!"

Shooks are laser-focused on a single, big message, and the good news is a shook and working with me solves both of these problems. It gives your targeted reader a single-focus book, which can be read quickly and easily thereby giving them the sense of accomplishment we all get when we finish a task we started (this is an "invisible" but important benefit of a shook).

It gives you a simple formula to craft content that is focused, powerful and in less time than required by traditional-length books. Shooks are a win-win for your reader and you!

Even though we are not focused on becoming a *New York Times* bestseller, there have been short books on the list over the years, most notably *Who Moved My Cheese?* and *The One Minute Manager*. The former has 96 pages and sold 28 million copies from 1998–2017 and the latter has 111 pages and sold 13 million copies in 10 years. The list of classic fictional short books is a long one, with *A Christmas Carol* and *Of Mice and Men* on it.

Never underestimate the power of short books and in many situations—*less can mean more.*

If today's consumer wants information in shorter, bite sized chunks, why not give it to them in a way that makes it easier for them to consume? Trying to fight this growing trend is futile and learning how to adapt to make it work for you is critical. This is the essence of what it means to be a Main Street Author and being able to leverage the power and prestige of being a published author in your community.

The very real benefit of being able to add the title of "author" to your credentials elevates your status and increases your perceived worth, which means you can become the *go-to* choice in your community for what you do. By simply promoting your shook as a helpful tool in your advertising and marketing, you can cut through the noise of most traditional advertising and marketing.

As a Main Street Author, you will be a bright, illuminating beacon of hope, help and guidance, and by crafting your book as a shook, you make it more likely to be read in its entirety, giving you a better chance readers will complete your call-to-action and eventually become a customer.

If there is only one thing you take away from reading this shook, it should be just how important I think it is for you to author your first shook, targeted at helping your ideal customer with bite size chunks of helpful information.

If you have already authored a book, you can use what I am about to share to re-focus on building a book-centric marketing strategy.

"I love the concept of shooks because not only are they easy to write, much easier to write for us as authors, but it means the people who are reading them are more likely to get through them. I've already have my manuscript sent out to about 15 of my clients as a bit of a 'testing.' Every one of them said 'Hey, I was able to get to the end,' and that's the magic of shooks!"

—Nigel Moore, author of
Package Price Profit

CHAPTER 2

WHAT MAKES A SHOOK SPECIAL?

In four words—SPEED AND INTENTIONAL DESIGN. Shooks are faster to create, faster to read and are "built" according to a unique and intentional design formula.

As I've previously mentioned, "shook" is short (no pun intended) for "short, helpful book." It is my trademarked description of a specific book format I have perfected which has a specific goal, content structure, physical size and page count. You can create print, digital and audio shooks. With this in mind, let me describe why I think shooks are special.

Shooks Invite Readership

Since the most obvious difference between a typical printed standard business book and a shook is the size, let me start by describing what makes a shook, a shook. Printed shooks are professionally printed, perfect bound paperback books. They are similar in quality to the types of books you buy on Amazon or at a local bookstore, and they are designed and formatted by professional book cover and interior designers, so they look and feel great.

Rather than the 5.5"x8.5" or 6"x9" trim size of typical business books, most shooks are intentionally designed to be 5.06"x7.81" in size, making them slightly smaller and therefore different-looking than other books (pocket shooks have a 4.4"x6.8" trim size). This size creates a "pattern interrupt" when you hand a prospect your shook because it's different from what they are used to. Today, appearing new, fresh and different is a smart strategy to get noticed, which is why shooks are designed the way they are.

Instead of the *"There is no way I am going to read that"* response many people have when they get a standard book, a shook's size invites them to read.

This smaller size also makes your shook easy to carry, share with others, mail and display. I keep several copies of my shooks in my car and in my laptop bag, so I always have them on hand to give away when I meet business owners and potential prospects for my business. My shook is my business card.

Shooks Are Physically Easier to Read

Shooks are designed to be physically easier to read for the average person. I don't know about you, but as I get older, reading printed text either on paper or on a screen is getting harder. Most designers do not worry about the physical readability of books, marketing and advertising materials, which is a big mistake. Instead of using design criteria and typography which are easier on the eye, they use a hard-to-read layout and hard-to-read fonts.

Remember, if a person cannot easily read your content, there is a high probability they will simply give up trying. For years, I have been preaching about the importance of making everything you create easy to physically read. The design of the words you are reading at this very moment are not just some default setting I merely used. The font choice, size and line spacing I am using in *Main Street Author* are the result of a study I did with people on my email list, where I asked them to review eight different standard book font and line spacing combinations.

What you are seeing on this page is the #1 "easiest to read" shook design layout. The good news is if you work with me, you don't have to worry about all these details. I take care of everything.

Shooks Are Faster to Read

Most business books have somewhere between 30,000–50,000 words, with many exceeding 75,000 words. They tend to be at least 200 pages and often can reach 300 to 400 pages. They take the average reader hours, if not days and weeks, to read from cover to cover, and while my bookshelf is filled with these traditional types of business books, I wanted shooks to be different. I am not saying the world doesn't need these types of longer books, I am just saying certain people would be better served publishing a shook instead of a book.

Shooks typically contain 12,000–15,000 words and have between 80–128 pages, but don't forget these are smaller pages, so they are faster to read and can be read by an average-speed reader in an hour or two. This means you can have an hour or two of "quiet time" with your readers, where they are focused on your message and getting to know you and how you can help them better.

Shooks Are Focused

Shooks are written for a specific and targeted reader, typically the type of person who would be an ideal customer for your business, and if you could wave a magic wand would be able to find hundreds if not thousands of similar people.

If you decide to personally work with me to develop your shook, one of the first things we will work on together is the identification of the reader you want to attract, help and eventually turn into a customer. This is a critical first step and one that provides a framework for the shook's content and promotion.

Shooks Are Easier to Understand

Shooks are helpful bite sized chunks of information your target reader is looking for. They are not meant to be the "complete and final" word on a topic. Instead, they contain highly focused content that offers helpful information, insights, tips, ideas, etc., on a topic.

Rather than teach a reader everything about the topic, shooks enlighten readers with your unique knowledge, expertise and opinions and then extend an invitation to get more from you as part of the "next step." If your subject requires lengthy text, my suggestion is to consider a series of shooks instead of one long, traditional book.

Shooks Offer Additional Information

Shooks are interactive and have various opportunities for readers to get valuable bonuses and extend the power of the shook with online content. This allows readers to get more helpful information and gives you the opportunity to capture their contact information, thereby building a follow-up database.

Shooks Get Readers to Raise Their Hand

Shooks have a clear "next step" call-to-action to get interested readers to self-identify. When people read your shook, there's a high probability you will have intrigued them and provided value and reason to take the next step, whatever that is for your sales process. Working together, we will uncover this next step and incorporate it clearly in your shook.

Publishing a Shook Solves
Two Stumbling Blocks

Most books are never written by qualified people who should write them because of two primary reasons—fear and time. Let me address both and put your mind at ease. Shooks are not meant to be works of literary art and perfection. Many people have the unnecessary fear their content and writing are not good enough to be in a book. This is hogwash, and if you can have a helpful and meaningful in-person conversation, you can publish a shook.

Your shook is an extension of you and how you talk and communicate. You want readers to feel as if you are sitting with them having a conversation and not a lecture. This means your shook will be written like you talk, and while every measure should be taken to ensure there are no obvious spelling, grammar and structure mistakes, this is not the ultimate goal.

You've heard the cliché, "People buy from people they know, like and trust," which means your shook needs to be helpful, empathetic and focused on the readers' wants and needs. It also needs to sound like it was written for a friend and should have an authentic, conversational "me to you" tone.

If we work together to publish your shook, I will make sure your content is polished and will be something you'll be proud to say, "I wrote this for you."

The other reason most books are never written is because of time and the mistaken notion that authoring a book has to take months or even years to complete. If you ever decide to work with a traditional publisher, it could take months or years to complete your book because of the editorial control publishers exert on authors.

Again, this is not what publishing a shook is all about, and slow authors don't get any special recognition or awards.

Recently, different companies have popped up offering you the chance to create your book in a few hours or talk your book out in a day. While these services may offer you a suitable path to getting your book done, the shook publishing process goes deeper into the design and architecture of the content. This is not about writing a book but instead crafting a well -thought-out and choreographed customer-attraction asset for your business.

My Main Street Author Programs, where you work <u>directly</u> with me to get your shook done and ready to be printed in as little as 8–12 weeks, are my proven, step-by-step publishing programs designed specifically for local business owners and the business owners who serve them.

It's my belief a business book you can be proud of takes longer than a few hours to create but shouldn't take more than two to four months to complete from concept inception to final printing. You can read more about working with me at the end of this shook.

CHAPTER 3

7 SMART REASONS TO PUBLISH YOUR SHOOK

A s I mentioned before, this shook is not intended to convince you of all the reasons why you should become a book author. There are many books which focus on all the smart reasons why you should want to add the title of "author" to your credentials, so I am not going to bog you down with what you probably already know. Instead I want to focus on the smart reasons I believe business owners should become shook authors and why they are so relevant to your type of business.

1. Creating and Publishing a Shook Is Fast

By their very nature of being a short book, shooks are much faster to create and don't require you to labor for years to publish. Plus, if you work with me, I will guide you and lead you along a path to get your shook done fast and without the hassle of doing it alone. Time is money, and the faster you can get your shook published, the more money you stand to make.

2. Authoring a Shook Positions You and Your Business Above Your Competition

If you're one of the types of business owners I described in the beginning of this shook, I believe helping before selling is absolutely essential. Shooks minimize the buying fear and concerns your prospects have by showing your empathy and concern for their well-being and success. This caring attitude and the fact you went through the effort of publishing a book for them will distinctly set you and your business apart from the competition. This puts you in the enviable "category of one" position for what it is you sell and do.

There's also a high probability your competition is not using a book to guide and help their prospects and market their products/services. In my 25 years of being in the professional marketing game and working with thousands of business owners, I've seen only a few dozen leverage the power of being a published author to create their own unique and distinct difference. Those that do, immediately distinguish themselves and create an enviable level of influence and authority.

3. Shooks Are Seen as Objects of Value

In a world inundated with free and (often) sloppy information, a printed shook with your name on it commands attention, respect and positions you as an expert authority on the subject. There is truly something magical that happens when you hand a person your shook and you see their expression change as they realize "you wrote the book" on the topic they are interested in at the moment.

Printed books are considered as valuable sources of information and valued in society. Books are sold in stores and online, and people expect to pay for information contained in a book. The bottom line is, building your marketing and advertising around a printed shook is an immediate and profitable game changer.

4. Shooks Position You as an "Author-ity"

It's interesting to note the word "authority" starts with "author." Being known as an authority and a person with something to say is critical these days because getting attention is harder than ever before. The good news is that a professionally designed and attractive shook cuts through the clutter and will get the attention of your ideal prospect.

Being the author of a shook gives you the platform to claim your position as the expert on your topic in your town (or around the world). The more you share your shook with prospects and media, the more well-known and famous you'll be for what you know.

5. Shooks Enable You to Attract Informed, Affluent Buyers

Depending on what you sell, attracting an educated prospect may be critical, and no other marketing or sales strategy does a better job of this than by being the author of your own shook. If your prospects are affluent and high value, they expect you to be unique. Using a shook as the keystone for your advertising, marketing and sale efforts is the right "bait" and enables you to attract these consumers.

6. Dollar for Dollar, a Shook Is the Most Powerful Customer-Attraction Asset You Can Create

Using books as a way to attract and get target leads to self-identify (by requesting the book) is a time-tested and proven strategy that goes back over 100 years. In my own research, I have found print ads from the Ostermoor Mattress Company that were used in the early 1900's and offered the free book, *The Test of Time*, to describe the unique benefits of their mattresses.

The advertisement states the book is, "144 pages of vital importance to anyone who values health and long life, and the restful sleep that insures both. Your name and address on a postal will do." This is classic lead-generation advertising at its finest.

Print advertisements from Ostermoor & Co.

Fast forward a few decades and Charles Atlas offered his book, *Everlasting Health and Strength*, to help "weaklings" become "new men." Example after example of using books as lead-generation tools can be found over the past decades right up to today, where books are still being offered on TV, Facebook and radio.

Why?

Because they are excellent and effective ways to attract the types of leads you're looking to attract. In Part II, I will share several different ways to use your shook as an effective customer-attraction asset.

7. Shooks Are Publicity and Media Magnets

With just a little effort, your shook can help you get in front of the media who may write articles, interview you or feature you on radio or TV. Today's media outlets are looking for real and valuable stories to share, and your shook could be just the thing their audience would be interested in hearing about.

In my opinion, every shook author should be making the effort to get their shook in front of targeted media (e.g., local or industry-related), which is why if we work together; part of my service is to develop a simple and effective PR strategy to announce your shook and why it's important for your intended target audience. The value of media exposure can be priceless, and one simple article or interview that came about because of your shook could make a huge difference in your business.

CHAPTER 4

12 SHOOK IDEAS TO CONSIDER PUBLISHING

I want you to clear your head of what you think it means to be an author. For years, I incorrectly understood what it meant to be an author, and if you think you must slave for months over your computer, cranking out every word of a traditional-style book to be an author, you are mistaken.

When I say I want you to be a shook author, it means I want you to be the author of the concept and big idea behind the shook and not necessarily the person who has written every word. I want you to focus on a problem your target reader has and show him or her how you can fix it, and there is no better way to accomplish this than with the unique positioning tool of your very own shook.

To get you thinking about the type of shook you can author, in this section I'm sharing 12 different shook ideas, some of which are more traditional and some of which you may have never considered.

Please realize this is not the be-all and end-all list of types of shook opportunities, but it lists the ones I believe are the most appropriate for business owners to consider publishing.

My goal is to get you thinking about what type of shook may be the best for you and your business. It may be one of these 12, or it may be another type of shook.

1. "Pocket" Shook

A "Pocket" shook is exactly what it sounds like—an even smaller and shorter shook that literally can fit into a pocket or purse. I have used this format for several projects, and it's an excellent format if your content is relatively brief and the concept of portability is important (e.g., an auto repair shook that is intended to be stored in a vehicle's glove compartment). These shooks are 4.4"x6.8" and their size makes them quite unique-looking and attention-grabbing.

2. "Compilation" Shook

The "Compilation" shook is ideal if you have a number of customer success stories. You can compile them into this type of shook where the stories "sell" you and your business. I used this strategy to create a fundraising shook for an organization that helps disadvantaged kids get into college. We had a number of kids write a short letter about the impact of the organization in their lives and then turned them into a shook. We raised over $100,000 by sending the shook out to potential donors.

3. "Essential Guide" Shook

The "Essential Guide" shook can be similar to the "how to" type of shook and useful when the focus of your shook is fairly technical and requires a more in-depth level of writing. I like to encourage my clients who use this format to "chunk" their information into 5–7 bite sized chunks and focus each chunk in its own chapter. This makes it much easier for the reader to understand and read through. My shook client, Nigel Moore, did an excellent job with this type of shook when he published, *Package Price Profit.*

4. "How to" Shook

The "How to" shook is a good one if your product or service is complicated or you want to "teach" a specific strategy. My SMART Publisher client, Julie Steinbacher, and I have created the *"You're Not Alone"* series of shooks with the first shook focused on the person who has been diagnosed and the second shook focused on the person caring for the patient. Julie is using these shooks in her practice, and together we have licensed them to a number of elder care attorneys around the country.

5. "Survival Guide" Shook

The "Survival Guide" shook is a good choice when your shook is focused on helping to make a frustrating and confusing topic less stressful and simple to fix. My shook client, Adam Weber, did exactly this when he published *The Appraisal Review Survival Guide*, which breaks down the complex steps for conducting commercial real estate appraisals with his own unique system.

A New and Exciting Way
to *Think About Medicare* and
Get the Benefits You Deserve

MEDICARE

MADE-TO-ORDER

MATTHEW PETRUSO
President of Benefit Advisors Insurance Group

6. "Mistakes to Avoid" Shook

This shook could be written pretty much by any type of business owner, and it's one where you outline and address the common mistakes people make when buying/using your product/service. My shook client and insurance agent, Matthew Petruso, created his first shook when he published *Medicare Made-to-Order*. This shook outlines several mistakes to avoid when navigating the confusing world of Medicare.

7. "Secrets" Shook

You've undoubtedly seen "Secrets of" and "Secrets to" type books. Everybody wants to know what the secrets are, so authoring a secrets shook about things that are known and not-so-well-known about your product/service could be a wise choice. My Main Street Author client, Amir Siddiqui, used this format when he wrote *Million Dollar Fitness Secrets*. In this shook, he shared his own specific strategies and secrets for obtaining a fitter and healthier body and life.

8. "Tips" Shook

The "Tips" type of shook is one of the easiest shooks for business owners to create since they are essentially a collection of pithy and powerful tips your targeted reader would find helpful concerning your products and services. Jeff Giagnocavo published a tip shook for mattress retailers when he started with one of my "Bite Sized Books" and authored *77 High Impact Low Budget Tips to Sell More Mattresses Easily*. He also created an industry-specific cover/version for an event he was speaking at (shown above).

9. "Big Idea" Shook

If you've developed a "Big Idea" that presents a new and unique way of doing something, creating this type of shook may be the perfect positioning tool for you and your business. My longtime client, the late Dr. Kevin Flood, created a shook around the Big Idea of how "silver" amalgam fillings contain dangerous mercury and should be removed, when he published *Are Your Teeth Toxic?*

10. "Go to Expert" Shook

The "Go to Expert" shook is the type of shook that should be used when positioning the focus on the author is the most important goal. This type of shook would typically be used by business owners who run a *personality-driven* business, where he or she is the unique selling proposition. My shook client, Sukuma Avery, who is a tradeshow performer, authored *The Magic of Tradeshowmanship* to help him differentiate himself from everybody else who provides the same service he does.

11. "Manifesto" Shook

If you have a unique philosophy or mission statement you want people to understand, a manifesto-style shook is a good choice. My *High Impact Marketing Manifesto* outlines the principles and rules of High Impact Marketing and what makes it different from "traditional" small business marketing. This type of shook is especially good if you want to present a contrarian point of view.

12. "Licensable" Shook

This is a unique type of shook and for the right person could be a nice profit center. The goal is to craft a shook to license to other people who do what you do. Essentially, you are creating the content/shook for others to put their name on, and my SMART Publisher Program makes this easy and fast. SMART Publisher, Julie Steinbacher, created a series of shooks for her law firm and then leveraged them further by offering them to her lawyer clients as licensable short books to use in their practice.

CHAPTER 5

SIMPLE TIPS TO WRITE YOUR SHOOK

If you have something important to say or can help others with your products or services, I believe you must share your ideas with the world by becoming a Main Street Author. I want you to get your shook done and done soon. As I have said several times previously, my shook-publishing process is the fastest and easiest way to get your shook done. However, any type of book you decide to author starts with you and getting your thoughts, ideas, opinions, etc., out of your head and onto the printed page.

In the previous chapter, I shared 12 different shook "models" you can use as a starting point for your shook. Which type of shook to create will be up to you, or if you decide to work with me, we'll figure out which of these options works best for you. These content creation options are in my personal preferred order.

1. Write It

The traditional method of writing your shook's content is, in my opinion, the best way to create your shook if you enjoy writing and are decent at it. I get that it can feel like a daunting task, but I believe sitting down and actually writing your content will pay off in many different ways in your business. You will see holes in your messaging and develop new and better ways to describe your solutions. No other person is as passionate and interested in your topic as you are, so if you can set time aside and use this shook as your blueprint, I know you can do it.

I literally shut myself in my office for a single day and crafted most of the content for this shook. Of course, I had properly outlined my thoughts and planned before sequestering myself, but I was able to complete most of this shook's content in a single, focused day. I am not saying you need to do the same thing, but there is something powerful about getting away from your day-to-day distractions to make yourself exceptionally productive.

Another option is to commit to writing 750 words a day, five days a week. Again, if you have properly outlined and planned your shook, this strategy will take you about five weeks to complete your shook content by only writing 750 words a day, five days a week. You should be able to craft 750 words in about

30–60 minutes, and on certain days you may be able to write 1,000 or even 1,500 words effortlessly. The more you write, the easier it becomes.

2. Present It

If you do face-to-face presentations or even virtual webinar-based talks, your 60-minute presentation could make the perfect content for your shook. The skills necessary to craft a compelling presentation, including the flow and content, are the same skills needed to create a good shook. Essentially, you deliver your presentation, record it and then have it transcribed so that it can be edited into its final format by you or a writer.

3. Talk It

Another book-authoring strategy which is popular these days is to talk your book out on your smart phone or computer, have it transcribed and then polished by a professional writer. For some, it might be easier to talk your shook out instead of sitting down at a computer. There are several online services for transcription which make this once expensive and tedious task much easier.

TIP: Check out Rev.com for a recommended transcription service I use.

4. Repurpose It

If you have lots of content you've previously written, you can repurpose it for your shook, saving you hours of time and energy. For example, if you have been writing blog content for years, you can take selected blog posts and use them as the main content of your shook. You could also convert videos and podcasts you have recorded into useable content.

5. Hire It

A final strategy and one I used to create the compilation book, *Dream Inc.*, was to find and hire a professional ghostwriter to interview each of the 29 contributors and write their chapter based on the interview content. You could hire a ghostwriter to interview you and write your shook's content.

The good news is that whichever path you decide to take will be super-fast because a shook contains a fraction of the word count found in traditional business books.

CHAPTER 6

SIMPLE TIPS TO DESIGN YOUR SHOOK

W hen it comes to designing your shook's interior and cover, you have several options available, but in my professional opinion, there is really only one choice that makes sense, assuming you want a shook to be proud of when displaying and giving to prospective customers. Like with anything in life, you only get one chance to make a good first impression, and an incorrectly designed shook is worse than no shook at all. So please keep that in mind as you consider your shook's interior and cover design. With that said, here are five tips for designing your shook.

1. Do-It-Yourself Templates

A quick search on the Internet will reveal several sources that sell Microsoft Word templates for creating your shook interior and various design templates for creating your cover. Unless you have a decent eye and patience for design, I do not recommend trying to design your own shook. Trust me, it will never look as good as it should, but if you insist on going this route, check out BookDesignTemplates.com.

2. Do-It-Yourself Software

There are several software packages you can purchase that will help you design your shook, including Scrivener and Kindle Create. Again, a word of caution—unless you are experienced at good design, I do not recommend you doing this yourself.

3. Work with a Book Designer

This option is the only option I recommend to anybody who is truly serious about publishing a high-quality shook. Effective book design requires an experienced designer who is familiar with what good book design consists of. Trust me, there are more things than you want to know. You should leave the design of your shook to a professional. Again, a search on the Internet for "book designer" or visiting sites like Guru.com or Upwork.com will give you options. Of course, you can always work with me and my team of professionals to create a shook you can be proud of!

BONUS: I share my best design tips and different ways you can print your shook in the companion training that is included with your copy of *Main Street Author*. Get it at MainStreetAuthor.com/gifts.

CHAPTER 7

MAIN STREET AUTHOR MARKETING STRATEGIES

U nlike other types of businesses, Main Street business owners have book-marketing needs and opportunities <u>unique</u> to their local business, which many book-marketing experts gloss over in their "*how to author a book*" books and services; and if they do describe or offer some sort of book marketing strategy it's typically not ideal for the Main Street business owner who wants to attract new customers in his or her <u>local</u> community.

This goal requires a different approach and must leverage shook-centric marketing tools like those found in my SMART Toolkit. SMART stands for **S**hook **M**arketing **A**dvantage **R**esults & **T**actics and this unique set of marketing tools are specifically designed for Main Street Authors.

When you leverage these tools and implement a shook-centric marketing system, your shook becomes the keystone and focus for your marketing and advertising efforts.

Your goal is to promote your shook and not your business, and while this may sound a bit odd, let me explain what I mean. Your shook is designed to attract certain types of people—your potential ideal customers—therefore you should start all initial "conversations" by offering your shook as the answer to what they want.

In your offline conversations, use your shook in your various advertising media, at prospect meetings, at events and in what I call WOW! Packages.

In your online conversations, offer your shook on your website either in its entirety or just a few chapters as a sampler (with an offer to get the complete shook). It can also be part of a digital information kit you send to qualified prospects, etc.

Because shooks follow a specific formula, they are designed to attract your targeted readers, get them to begin to know, like and trust you, and invite them to contact you as an interested prospect.

The "promotion" of your business happens organically with a shook. You don't need to be using the same old lines and tired strategies others in your industry use to try to get attention and make a sale. When people read and engage with your shook, they are buying into you and your business and are pre-sold on doing business with you.

On the next pages, I will share several SMART Toolkit examples.

Yours Tribally,

Nigel Moore

Leader of <u>The Tech Tribe</u>
Author of <u>Package Price Profit</u>

p.s. Connect with me on <u>Facebook</u> & <u>LinkedIn</u>

Add "Author" to Your Title

Most business owners never publish a real book, which automatically puts those that do in a valuable and prestigious "club." Make sure you add the title "Author of YOUR BOOK TITLE" to your email signature, business cards, biography, social media descriptions, etc. The more places you can feature your shook and you as the author of it, the better your chances for getting the right people to see it and want it.

In Your Place of Business

Featuring your shook in your store, office or place of business (assuming prospects visit you) is smart. I have had clients create "shook racks" like the one in the photo above, which allow visitors to take a copy. Others have created a point-of-sale rack where they sell their shook to visitors.

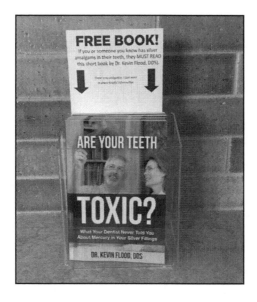

Strategic Business Partner Display

This is one of the smartest and most effective ways for a local Main Street Author to get their book in front of the right prospect. The strategy is to give strategic business partners copies of your shook to display and give to their customers. Main Street Author, Dr. Kevin Flood, worked with several local business partners, and because he is a holistic dentist, displaying his shook in health food stores, chiropractor offices and similar businesses enabled him to attract many new patients.

In Direct Mail Campaigns

Creating a direct mail campaign where you either offer your shook as a call-to-action (e.g., the person receiving your letter must request the shook) or where you include your shook as part of the mailing package is an effective way to use your shook to advance the conversation. One of the strategies I personally use and encourage my clients to use is to send your shook in a small, padded gold envelope and use the theme of the value of gold and the "gold nuggets of wisdom" (found in the shook) in the cover letter.

In WOW! Packages

I call them WOW! Packages—and you may have heard them referred to as "shock and awe" packages. Regardless, this is a strategically designed marketing asset, which is used to get attention and WOW the person receiving it. I have gone as far as printing my own full-color boxes which are sized exactly for my shooks and related marketing materials. This is an effective way to building a fun and attention-grabbing kit around your shook.

Local Media Interviews & Articles

Once you are a published author, who is focused on helping your fellow community residents, you have a great opportunity to attract local media attention. This means free exposure if they pick up your story. With a very small budget and campaign, my daughter got a bunch of online and offline articles about her shook, *Dog Joy*. She was featured on the front page of several local newspapers and was even in a feature article in a local magazine. This exposure helped her raise thousands of dollars for dog rescues.

Local Display Advertising

Wherever you are doing lead-generation advertising, you can and should use your shook as the call-to-action. My shook client and Medicare expert, Matt Petruso, created a roadside billboard where he featured his shook, *Medicare Made-to-Order,* quite predominately. You can do the same thing in your print ads, phone book ads, newsletters, delivery vehicle wraps, Little League field banners, etc.

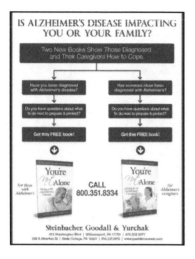 

Print Advertising

Creating shook-centric print advertisements is an effective way to get the word out about your shook. Typically, we create several different print ad sizes, including quarter-page, half-page and full-page ads, which all follow classic direct-response marketing principles. You can place these ads in your own media (e.g. newsletter) or in local newspapers, magazines, coupon mailers, restaurant menus—whatever your potential ideal readers are looking at.

Advertorials

Advertorials are a unique type of print advertisement and a smart strategy to market your shook. Designed to look like an article, these information-rich ads articulate why you wrote your shook, who it's for and why they want to read it. It ends with a strong and clear call-to-action to get your shook.

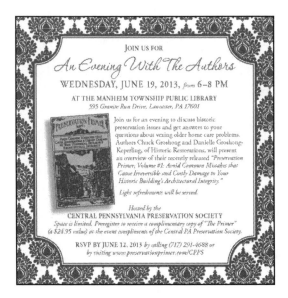

An Evening with the Author

Once you become a published Main Street Author, it automatically differentiates you and positions you in a new light as a local expert and authority. You can and should capitalize on this unique position. A powerful strategy is to create a local event and then market it as *An Evening with the Author* to get attention and differentiate it. Your event could be a simple meet-and-greet or go deeper with some in-depth training on your shook's primary topic.

Tradeshows & Events

Doing lead-generation marketing at events where you are exhibiting is a smart strategy for building a list and identifying ideal prospects. Because of its eye-catching size and appearance, attendees will stop and want a copy of your shook. I like to use a simple, three-question survey in return for a free copy because it allows me to collect important data for follow-up after the event. Few business owners use a book at an event this way, which gives you a smart lead-generation advantage.

Local Networking Events

If you actively participate in local networking groups and events, using your shook as a business card and featured giveaway can be an effective way to get your shook into the hands of ideal readers or referral partners. Forget boring business cards and the ubiquitous tri-fold brochure everybody else is using. When you meet an ideal prospect and hand him or her your shook, the magic starts to happen. Don't be surprised when people ask you to autograph it!

Employees & Customer Referrals

Another shook-marketing strategy that is unique to local Main Street Authors is the ability to have their employees and existing customers distribute their shooks for them. Ask employees to give your shook to people they know and can benefit from what you offer. Create a monthly contest for employees and award prizes for the person who generates the most new business. Create a new customer welcome page with copies of your shook and instructions on how to give it away as a referral tool.

Local TV & Radio Spots

You've probably seen TV spots and heard radio spots where the commercial featured a free book as the device to get a response. If you do any sort of television or radio advertising, creating a shook-centric promotion can be very effective. Remember, promote the shook—not your business. You want people watching or listening to want to get it. Then make sure you offer simple and clear directions to get it—typically a short web URL and phone number.

Shook Website

Creating a shook-specific page on your current website or even an entire shook-specific website is an effective way for people to find your shook online. My suggestion is to offer to send the printed shook at no cost or "free but pay for shipping." You can also create a PDF sampler of your shook and use that as an opt-in download (don't send the entire shook). Then use the page link or website URL in your lead-generation marketing.

Online Videos

If you use video in your business marketing, you have an excellent platform to announce and promote your shook. The visual benefits allow you to show your shook, thumb through it and easily explain how and why to get a copy. Immediately after his shook was published, Mathew Petruso launched an online campaign announcing its availability on YouTube.

Social Media Posts & Advertising

Announcing and advertising your shook on the social media platforms of your choice is a targeted and effective way to promote a "Free Book" offer. Remember, you are not looking to sell your shook, you simply want to get it in front of the right audience and motivate them to request a copy. The targeted advertising strategies of Facebook and other local websites allow you to get your shook in front of very specific audiences.

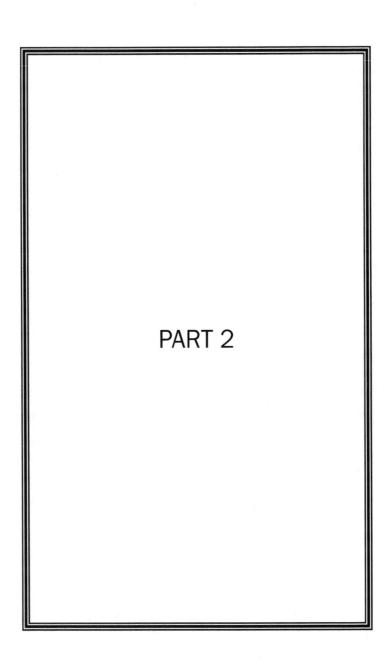

PART 2

SHOOK BUILDING BLOCKS

"Our goal is to become the premier law firm in our area for Alzheimer's planning. The shooks that we are giving to giving to clients and our referral sources and offering through our local newspaper are creating a positive stir. We are being told that no one else is doing this—they are a great differentiator and helps position us as the go-to resource in our community for this area of the law."

—Tiffany O'Connell author of
You're Not Alone shooks

CHAPTER 8

THE SHOOK "SPECIAL SAUCE"

A s I have said before, there are two big differentiators that make a shook a shook and a worthy alternative to publishing a traditional book to use to attract more ideal customers.

Speed.

Intentional design.

Shooks are meant to be created faster by you and read faster by your prospects.

My shook "special sauce" is what makes this all possible, easy and super-fast for you. Recently, I conducted a training for a group of business owners, and I thought my presentation slides and commentary would give you a "taste" of this special sauce.

While I would love the opportunity to work with you on all this (assuming we are a good fit), you can take this structure and use it yourself. Just remember, the fastest way to success is to have an experienced expert (e.g., a coach, consultant, advisor) to guide, prompt, question, challenge and encourage you. More details on how we can work together can be found in Part 3.

What Is Your Personal Goal?

- What is your personal BIG GOAL with your shook?

- What are you trying to accomplish?

- How will you know you have accomplished it?

- What metrics will you use to know if your shook is doing what you want it to do?

Shook Building Block 1

Building Block 1
What Is Your Personal Goal?

You need to know right from the outset what your primary goal of your shook is, and if you've read this far, you know it's not about selling it!

What are you looking to accomplish with your shook, and how will you know you have accomplished it? Most business owners I work with want to use their shook for two primary reasons:

1. To increase their influence and authority
2. To attract more of their ideal customers

What are your goals for your shook?

Identify Your Ideal Reader

- Identify your ideal reader.

- This should be your eventual ideal customer/client/patient.

- List any important demographics, psychographics, details we should keep in mind when crafting the book's content.

- If you can focus on one "type" of reader, the better.

Shook Building Block 2

Building Block 2
Identify Your Ideal Reader

The first step to outlining your shook is to identify your ideal targeted reader. Who do you want to read this book and become a customer?

This is the person you write your shook for and nobody else! Everything on and in your shook should be designed and written for this person so that when they get a copy, they say to themselves, "This book was written for me!"

This is a critical, must-do first step, so consider your ideal target reader carefully.

What Is Your Shook Hook?

- What is the BIG IDEA behind your shook?

- What is your big promise?

- How are you trying to help your readers?

- Why should anybody read your shook?

  —What BIG problem will your shook start to fix for your reader?

Shook Building Block 3

Building Block 3
What Is Your Shook Hook?

The hook of your shook is the Big Idea behind it and the reason you created the shook for your ideal and targeted reader.

Create a promise for your shook and explain to your reader how investing the time to read it will help them solve a problem or gain something they want.

Remember, nobody wants to read your shook until they understand what it's going to do for them and how it's going to make their life easier, better, etc.

Developing your shook hook is something we can work on together to make it special and enticing.

Your Shook Title & Subtitle

- What is your shook's title?

  —Keep the main title short and sweet—just a few words.

- What is your subtitle?

  —Expand on the title but try to keep to 10 words or less.

- Remember your shook title should deliver a clear and compelling benefit or worthy goal, etc.

Shook Building Block 4

Building Block 4
Your Shook Title & Subtitle

Crafting your shook's title and subtitle is an iterative and important process. It's similar to developing a strong headline when copywriting and requires time, work and rework to get it right.

The good news is if you've identified your targeted reader and your hook, creating an attention-grabbing title that practically forces people to want to read your shook is simple.

Personally, I am a fan of a short title and longer subtitle. Take a look at the cover of this shook to see an example of a good title that took several rounds of ideas to finalize.

Front Cover & Spine Details

- Front cover details

    —Visuals

    —Title and subtitle

    —Author(s)

    —Foreword by?

    —Starburst offer?

- Spine details

    —Title and author name

    —Logo?

Shook Building Block 5

Building Block 5
Front Cover & Spine Details

Your shook's front cover is where you get the opportunity to make a powerful first impression, and unless you are a graphic designer yourself, you want to let a professional create your shook cover. Using the right graphics, fonts and other details is critically important, and you don't want to be sloppy or cheap about this. Every business owner who works with me will get a professionally designed cover that will get the attention of your target reader and make your shook look great.

As far as the spine, you want to have your title and your name on the spine. Your goal is to make it easy to find your shook on a bookshelf.

Back Cover Details

- Back cover details

    —Book description and "what's inside" bullets

    —Price and category

    —Author bio

    —Website URL

    —ISBN and barcode

Shook Building Block 6

Building Block 6
Back Cover Details

The back cover is the final piece of the three parts of your shook cover (front, spine and back). Here is what I like to include on the back cover:

- Strong "reason to read" headline
- Shook description including a few specific "here's what's inside" bullets
- A short author bio and website
- ISBN and barcode
- Price and book category

Reader Bonus/Gift Offer

- This is your shook's "Passive Call-to-Action" and is the secondary action you want a reader to take.

- This one-page offer is designed to give the reader a valuable bonus/gift if they visit your website and exchange their contact information for free gift or call your business.

- This should be something of value that the reader would want.

- The offer should include a simple web URL for the reader to visit or phone number to call.

Shook Building Block 7

Building Block 7
Reader Bonus/Gift Offer

We've finally gotten to the first page of your shook. This is the right-hand side page that is first seen when somebody opens your shook. In many books this page is left blank or is the title page. In a shook this page is specifically designed to be a reader bonus/gift page where readers can get a valuable bonus/gift right away.

I call this the "Passive Call-to-Action," and it's the secondary thing you want a reader to do after reading your shook. I like this "passive" strategy because it shows you are willing to give additional value to your readers before they even start to read your shook and allows you to build a reader email database.

Also By Page

- **OPTIONAL FRONT MATTER PAGE.**

- If you have written/created other books, reports, trainings, etc., you should include them on this page.

Shook Building Block 8

Building Block 8
Also By Page

This is an optional page, but if you've created other books, reports, trainings, etc., you should include them on this page.

Title Page

- This page includes your title, subtitle and your name.

- It should be designed in such a way to give you an area for you to sign and personalize your shook.

Shook Building Block 9

Building Block 9
Title Page

Your title page includes your title, subtitle and name. I like to design this page so that it leaves room for you to write a personal note and sign your shooks when giving them out.

Testimonial Page(s)

- **OPTIONAL FRONT MATTER PAGE(S).**

- If you want to distribute pre-release copies of your shook to your inner circle, important people you know, customers, etc., for them to send you a shook testimonial you would include them on these pages.

- Testimonials should inspire others to read your shook.

- They should be short, sweet and specific.

Shook Building Block 10

Building Block 10
Testimonial Page(s)

This is an optional page, but if you have testimonials and reviews of your shook, you should include them here. The way you get them is to give out pre-release copies to specific individuals and ask them to write a short testimonial about the shook. Be strategic about who you ask to review.

My shook clients, Dr. Don Reid and Doug Brown, got a former client to become a current client again by simply asking him to review their shook. This wasn't their intention, but after reading the shook, the former client realized what he was missing and signed back up for their program.

Copyright Page

- Copyright ownership—typically you or your business name.
- Publisher information
  - —Optionally you can use your company or brand as the publisher.
- Any important legal information and disclaimers.
- Consider adding a date code to track shook versions.

Shook Building Block 11

Building Block 11
Copyright Page

This page includes all copyright information, disclaimers, publisher details and important legal information.

Dedication Page

- **OPTIONAL FRONT MATTER PAGE.**

- Your place to dedicate your shook to

    —Important person to you.

    —Group of people, industry, niche, etc.

Shook Building Block 12

Building Block 12
Dedication Page

This is an optional page, which allows you to dedicate your shook to an important person or persons, a group of people, specific niche, etc.

Acknowledgements Page

- **OPTIONAL FRONT MATTER PAGE.**

- Your place to acknowledge people who helped you.

Shook Building Block 13

Building Block 13
Acknowledgements Page

This is an optional page, which allows you to acknowledge and thank people who were helpful to you in creating your shook.

Table of Contents

- A Table of Contents is important to have and one of the most important part of a nonfiction book.

- Your section and chapter headings should be clear and inform the reader what's in store.

- A good table of contents tells the story of your shook.

Shook Building Block 14

Building Block 14
Table of Contents

The table of contents is an important part of your shook and should entice readers to want to read it. Make sure you check and double-check the titles and page numbers to make sure they are correct before going to print.

Foreword

- **OPTIONAL FRONT MATTER PAGE.**

- If you can get a notable person to write the foreword for your shook, this can be quite powerful.

- Optionally, you can have a customer write it, etc.

- The idea is to have a third-party endorsement of your shook.

Shook Building Block 15

Building Block 15
Foreword

This is an optional page, but if it makes sense and you can find a V.I.P. to write the foreword to your shook, it can make it that much more powerful. When thinking about a person to write it, consider who you would like to have associated with your shook and who may be inclined to share it with their circles of influence simply because they were asked to write the foreword. If you cannot find a notable V.I.P., consider asking a valuable customer to write it for you.

Who Should Read This Book?

- **OPTIONAL FRONT MATTER PAGE.**

- If you want to connect even more, while also repelling others, you can include this section where you are specific about who should read the book (and who shouldn't).

- This is a bold strategy, but it can strengthen the bond with your target reader.

Shook Building Block 16

Building Block 16
Who Should Read This Book?

This is an optional section but one I personally like to include, like I did in this shook. I like to be upfront and transparent with my shook's goals and exactly who I created it for. While I appreciate people, who are interested in my shook, if they don't fit the profile of the types of business owners I'm looking to attract and work with, they do me little good.

This section allows me to boldly proclaim who should and should not read my shook. In turn, this will strengthen the bond with my target readers, since they know I wrote it specifically for them.

My Promise to You

- • OPTIONAL FRONT MATTER PAGE.

- • Starting your shook off with a bold promise is smart.

- • It keeps you focused on exactly what you need to convey in the shook and reminds you of its purpose.

- • It prepares your reader for what to expect in the pages to come and sets an important tone on how you conduct your business.

Shook Building Block 17

Building Block 17
My Promise to You

This is an optional page but one I believe you should include. Starting your shook off with a bold promise is a smart way to keep you focused on what you must deliver and prepare your readers for what to expect. Few business owners set any sort of lofty expectation these days, so making a promise from the beginning shows you are different than the masses.

Introduction

- Reason why intro.
- Here's what you'll discover in this shook.
- Here's why this is different.
- Why this is important to you now.
- Personal invitation to contact you.

Shook Building Block 18

Building Block 18
Introduction

I recommend all shook authors start their shook with a "reason why" introduction, which articulates the reason(s) why you are publishing it. Let your readers know what they will get by reading it, why it's different, and why it's important they read it now.

An excellent book recommendation for crafting your "why" is *Start with Why* by Simon Sinek. I found this book to be an excellent reminder when creating any type of marketing message.

Main Content

- These could be Chapters/Tips/Mistakes/Ideas/Secrets.

- Each of these body content chapters is the main content of your shook.

- These chapters are typically 1,500–2,500 words in length.

- I suggest somewhere between 5–7 content chapters total.

- Remember, you are creating "bite size" content chunks.

Shook Building Block 19

Building Block 19
Main Content

The main content section of your shook is where you include your Chapters/Tips/Mistakes/Ideas/Secrets. Remember, these are bite sized chunks of information focused on helping the reader with your shook hook. The typical length of these chapters is 1,500–2,500 words depending on how many you have. I usually try to limit the number of content chapters to no more than seven.

Remember, shooks are NOT meant to teach readers everything you know about the topic. They are meant to provide valuable information and then guide the reader to the next step, which is typically reaching out and contacting you.

The Next Step

- What is the "one thing" you want the reader to do?

- This is your "Active Call-to-Action" and is the main thing you want a reader to do after reading your shook

  —Typically, call your place of business or visit.

- Give explicit and detailed instructions on what to do next.

Shook Building Block 20

Building Block 20
The Next Step

It's critical your shook tells readers the next thing they must do in order to achieve the goal they were seeking when they first picked it up. I call this the "Active Call-to-Action," and it's *the* thing you want the reader to do after reading your shook.

I like to keep this limited to one thing, so it's clear and simple to do. Depending on your business, it could be to call you, visit you, fill out a survey, etc.

Give explicit and detailed instructions on what to do next if they truly want to solve their problem or achieve their goal.

Author Bio

• Your professional bio and important details, including:

— How long in business

— Why you got into this business

— Important awards, credentials, inventions, etc.

— Personal details

— Your personal website if you have one

— A professionally shot photograph

Shook Building Block 21

Building Block 21
Author Bio

Include your bio and important details about your background, experience, etc. This allows your readers to get to know you better. If you don't have professionally shot photographs and headshot photos, now is a good time to get them done. You can use one on your back cover and in your bio.

Author Resources

- **OPTIONAL BACK MATTER PAGE .**

- If you have other offerings you want to put in front of your readers, include them here.

Shook Building Block 22

Building Block 22
Author Resources

This is an optional page, but if you have other resources you would like readers to know about, include them in this page.

Reader Bonus/Gift Offer

- This is your shook's "Passive Call-to-Action" and is the secondary action you want a reader to take.

- This one-page offer is designed to give the reader a valuable bonus/gift if they visit your website and exchange their contact information for free gift or call your business.

- This should be something of value that the reader would want.

- The offer should include a simple web URL for the reader to visit or phone number to call.

Shook Building Block 23

Building Block 23
Reader Bonus Page

Depending on your shook's page count (all printed books should have a page count divisible by four— e.g., 104 pages, 108 pages, 112 pages, etc.), you may have a blank last even-numbered page. Rather than let this go to waste, I suggest repeating the same reader bonus/gift offer which started your shook like I did on the last page of this shook.

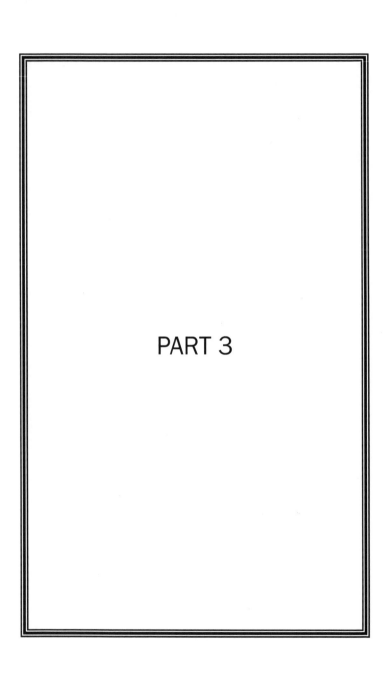

PART 3

MEET A FEW
MAIN STREET AUTHORS

"Mike Capuzzi is a man of integrity and exceptional insights and ideas. He also has that special character trait of actually doing what he says he is going to do. Finding key strategic partners for one's business is one of the surest and safest ways to growing and creating an even more successful business, and you cannot do wrong by partnering with Mike Capuzzi."

—Julie Steinbacher, author of the
You're Not Alone series of shooks

CHAPTER 9

JULIE STEINBACHER, ELDER LAW ATTORNEY

J ulie Steinbacher is an elder law attorney, with law offices in Williamsport and State College, PA. I have had the good fortune to know and work with Julie for over a decade, and what I admire most about her is her constant effort to always be marketing in powerful and unique ways.

Over the years, Julie has published several books to promote herself and her law practice, but none of them were specifically designed to be quickly read by a prospect and get them to "the next step." When she heard about the shooks I was publishing for others, she immediately scheduled a call with me to see how a shook could work for her lead-generation efforts.

Fast forward almost a year and Julie has authored two shooks, *You're Not Alone: Living with Alzheimer's disease* and *You're Not Alone: Living as an Alzheimer's Caregiver*, and is currently working on her third shook focused on dementia. She has also become a SMART Publisher and is leveraging her shooks in her coaching business and allowing her members to become shook authors.

The Challenge

Like any Main Street business owner, attracting new prospects and converting them into customers is a daily challenge. When she decided to focus more of her marketing efforts on specifically attracting clients affected by Alzheimer's disease, she knew she needed to take an information-first approach and help people understand the disease and how to cope and prepare.

She wanted something that would be fairly easy for her to produce, simple for her prospects to digest and effective, which is why she loved the concept of authoring a short, helpful book.

The Solution

Interestingly, during our initial calls together, we realized that she would be better served authoring two different shooks, one for the person suffering from the disease and one for the person who is the caregiver. This would allow her to have two distinct and helpful messages and specific follow-up campaigns. The entire process from idea generation to content creation to printed shooks took about 12 weeks and the results, as of the time I am writing this, are impressive.

Significant Results

In the first months of promoting her shooks, Julie has had 75 shook requests and has given many more away at her seminars and local events. They are an important first step in a fairly long sales process.

From this group of 75 (some of which were current clients), 10 people requested an initial consultation, and as of the date I am publishing this shook, six of the 10 have become new clients, which represent an initial value of over $40,000 to her firm. Julie fully expects to convert the others after a bit more follow-up with them.

This is the power of being a Main Street Author.

"I've been a client of Mike's for years and when he announced the opportunity to work with him to publish a short book, I immediately said yes because I know his level of professionalism and expertise are top-notch. Ironically, at the same time as his announcement, another book-publishing expert was trying to get me to work with her, but like I said, as soon as I found out Mike was offering this service, my decision was made."

—Dr. Kevin Flood, DDS, author of
Are Your Teeth Toxic?

CHAPTER 10

DR. KEVIN FLOOD, HOLISTIC DENTIST

Dr. Kevin Flood was a holistic dentist in Grand Rapids, MI, and as I was going to print with this shook, I found out he unexpectedly passed away. I first met Kevin back in 2008 and have worked with him since 2012 as both a mastermind group member and private client. His unique, holistic approach to dentistry was different than most traditional dentists and for years, he had created many outside-the-box marketing campaigns.

During a recent consulting day, Kevin told me he had always wanted to write a book but struggled getting his thoughts together and actually getting it done. He went on and said he had been at a recent event where a speaker was talking about the effectiveness of books as a marketing tool for dentists. He then pulled a book out of his bag, which the seminar speaker had authored on the topic of writing a lead-generation book in just a few days and handed it to me.

As I glanced through it, he said, "Mike, this made me laugh when I saw it," (apparently the promise of writing a book in only a few days struck him as funny). He went on to say, "There is no way I am going to work with this person. I want to work with you and publish a shook." In typical Kevin-fashion, he knew what he wanted and was able to make a quick decision to become a Main Street Author.

The Challenge

One of the unique aspects to Kevin's practice was his practice of mercury-free dentistry. If you have any silver fillings in your mouth, you unknowingly are exposing yourself to toxic mercury. Without getting into too much detail here, silver amalgam fillings are bad for you. When I found out about this a few years ago from another mercury-free dentist in my hometown, my wife and I immediately had all the silver fillings removed. But I digress.

The challenge of helping people understand the dangers of traditional amalgam fillings is an ideal focus for a short, helpful book and having gone through the awareness and removal process myself, I was excited to work with Kevin on his shook. Given what a new patient was worth to Kevin's practice, the investment in a shook was a no-brainer. So, we got started and Kevin began working on the content—it wasn't long before we encountered our second challenge.

The Solution

It quickly become apparent that even though Kevin is a decent copywriter and marketer, the challenge of sitting down and writing the contents of a shook, even with my explicit directions and guidance, was going to be more than he wanted to do. When I made the offer to write the shook for him, with his input and guidance, he immediately chose that path and within 45 days, *Are Your Teeth Toxic?: What Your Dentist Never Told You About Mercury in Your Silver Fillings* was published.

Significant Results

Kevin began using his shook in a variety of ways, including developing a shook website (see page 71). The smart strategy he leveraged was to work with a number of local strategic partners (e.g., chiropractor, health food store, wellness studio) to allow him to display and give away his shook in their place of business (see page 59). This enabled these other business owners to give Kevin's helpful shook as a valuable gift to their patients and customers.

During one of our follow-up calls, Kevin shared with me that within 30 days of implementing this simple strategy, three different individuals read his shook and became new patients. The potential lifetime value of these patients to Kevin was significant.

"I can say with 100% confidence, none of this would have happened had I not made that one small decision to seek out Mike Capuzzi. If you believe you and your business are destined for greater things and to have a bigger impact, Mike is a person you need to follow and do what he says."

—Jeff Giagnocavo, author of
*77 High Impact, Low Budget Tips to Sell
More Mattresses Easily*

CHAPTER 11

JEFF GIAGNOCAVO, MATTRESS RETAILER

J eff Giagnocavo is an independent mattress re-
tailer and consultant to other mattress retailers. His two stores are located in Lancaster, PA,
and if there is one thing I can tell you about Jeff it's
that he is a "marketer's marketer."

I've worked with Jeff for years and have been con-
stantly amazed at the marketing he and his business
partner, Ben McClure, create for their business, including their world-famous "Dream Room" and use
of a number of short books to help people make
smart buying decisions when it comes to buying a
mattress and bedding accessories.

The mattress retail industry has the same reputation as the used-car industry, which is why Jeff and
Ben's use of an "information-first" marketing strategy
is so unique. Their focus on building trust and creating a safe buying environment has created impressive
year-over-year growth and has resulted in Jeff being

a sought-after speaker and content contributor for the bedding industry. Even though Jeff uses short books in his retail business, what I want to share is his use of a shook as a means to attract other mattress retailers for his consulting business.

The Challenge

In 2017, Jeff had the opportunity to be a keynote speaker at an event hosted by the Specialty Sleep Association. He knew there would be several ideal potential clients in the audience and wanted to develop what is known as a "whale-hunting" strategy in the consulting world. This means creating a campaign whereby the small number of whales (big profit potential clients) identify themselves and want to work with you.

The keynote opportunity was a good one for Jeff, the only challenge was he had less than four weeks to prepare his presentation and strategy, so we put our heads together and came up with a plan.

The Solution

Given the fact Jeff loves shooks, we decided to implement a shook-centric campaign. Jeff's time was limited, so instead of crafting a new shook, I suggested he license one of my "60-Minute Shooks" which are licensable shooks I have created. My *77 High Impact Marketing Tips* shook was ideal for his efforts, and we proceeded to customize a few of the tips so they would be specific to mattress retailers. Editing a few pages versus writing an entire book made this easy and painless for Jeff.

We wanted to make sure every attendee received a copy of the shook, so we did two smart things to ensure this. The first is that we asked the president of the association to write the Foreword to the shook, which he agreed to. [SIDE NOTE: This strategy of having a V.I.P. write your shook's Foreword practically guarantees their support, endorsement and promotion of your shook.]

The second thing we did, which is simple these days with print-on-demand book printing, was to customize the shook's cover for the association (see page 44). Between having the president of the association write the Foreword and having a custom version for the event, there was no hesitation when we asked to put a copy of the shook on each audience member's chair.

Significant Results

Giving away his shook in this manner not only differentiated Jeff from other speakers but immediately resulted in two new consulting clients, each worth thousands of dollars per month, and several new members for his membership program.

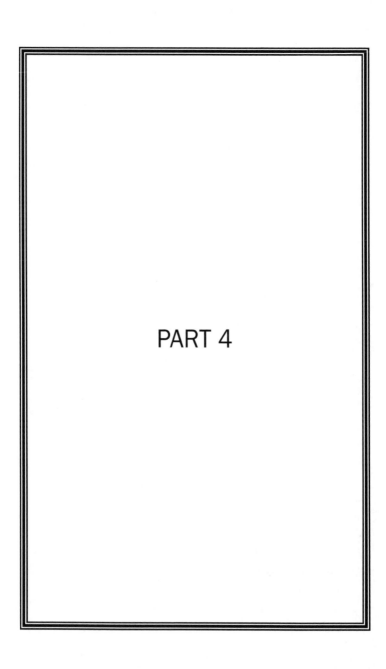

PART 4

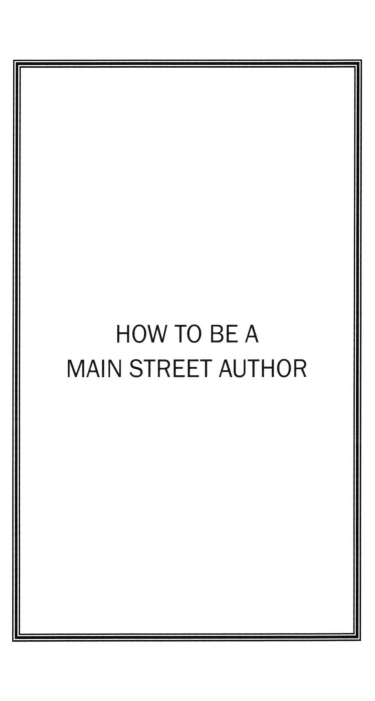

HOW TO BE A
MAIN STREET AUTHOR

"Mike really cares about the people he works with. We had calls every week to make sure that I was on the right path during the writing process, and when I went off the path at times, Mike got me right back on track. If I had questions or needed an idea, Mike was an email or call away and very responsive. Mike also kept me accountable in getting writing done. After each call, he would give me the next action step in what needed to be done for us to keep moving forward."

—Sukuma Avery, author of
The Magic of Tradeshowmanship

CHAPTER 12

SHOOK PUBLISHING OPPORTUNTIES

I hope by now you're convinced a shook is a must -have valuable asset for you and your business. As a matter of fact, I hope I have inspired you to think about multiple shooks you can create for your business—each addressing a specific issue you can help people with.

If you're still not convinced, I want you to consider what one new customer is worth to your business.

The bigger question is what your time is worth, and does it make sense for you to try to figure out all that's involved and do it alone? Or do you make the decision to work with an experienced marketing and publishing professional who will do everything in his power to ensure you publish a shook that makes you proud, and more importantly, attracts more ideal customers?

The fact of the matter is you have several options in front of you right now.

You can simply shelve this idea "for later."

You can start (or maybe restart) on your own and hope to get your shook done. Be aware this approach means you need to manage not only yourself but also an editor, proofreader, cover designer, interior designer, ebook designer and book printing company.

You can work with a low-end, "interview turned into book" publishing partner. You can think of this option like going to a national chain restaurant. You can get a meal, but is it really good, quality food?

You can work with an expensive, high-end, "agency-style" publishing partner and expect to pay $25,000 or more for this "privilege." This is like going to a high-end restaurant where you expect high-quality food (and usually get it), but you pay double or even triple of what the food should cost, simply to experience the brand.

I have several distinct shook publishing opportunities, and if you have read this far, I am sure one or more is ideal for you. These offerings include:

1. The Main Street Author Programs

2. The SMART Publisher Program

3. 60-Minute Shooks

I will describe each of these in further detail on the next few pages. Regardless of the path you take, you should know that when you work with me, in whatever capacity, you benefit from my two+ decades of experience, making sure you don't stall, trip or fumble. The reality is there are a bunch of places where you can make costly mistakes when publishing a book for your business. Considerable time should be given to the content, structure, goals and promotion of your shook, and this cannot be done in an hour or two, or even in a day. At least not in my opinion.

Rest assured, when we work together, you will get the best of me working for you, and you get an all-inclusive and personalized opportunity to get your shook done right and done fast. We will have scheduled phone calls, and you will have direct access to me, as I guide you step-by-step. Before you know it, you will be a Main Street Author and have a professionally published shook working for you and your business.

The Main Street Author Programs

The Main Street Author Programs are the "work directly with Mike to get my shook done" turnkey programs. Everything you need to get the content created and the shook published is included and on average it takes 8–12 weeks from start to finish. Each of these programs offers you direct access to my years of experience, and the guidance and accountability you need to get your shook done efficiently and correctly.

There are three Main Street Author Program options, including:

The Basic Publishing Program—This is for the local business owner who wants a simple, even shorter printed shook with a maximum of 100 pages.

The Local Publishing Program—This is for the local business owner who wants a longer, more comprehensive printed shook (max 128 pages) to use in his or her local community.

The Global Publishing Program—This is for the business owner who has a global audience, and who wants a printed shook, ebook shook and audio shook to sell on Amazon and other global retailers.

Regardless of which program you choose, the end result is that you will have your own short, helpful book published specifically for you and your business.

The SMART Publisher Program

If you are a coach, consultant or have a membership-driven group for Main Street business owners and want to leverage and license a *"done for you"* shook to your members, I've created a unique publishing program for you.

My SMART Publisher Program is a formal joint-venture where we create a shook or series of shooks on your focused topic and then allow your members or clients to license, personalize and use them in their own respective businesses. Your responsibility includes shook content development, marketing opportunities and sales. My company does everything else and manages the entire project.

This is such a unique and profitable venture I have written an entire shook about it. *WIN WIN WIN* describes all the benefits of having your own shook-publishing opportunity available for your members and how working with me will make this fast, simple and quite profitable for you. I believe offering a licensable shook to your members can be one of the smartest new things you can offer them to help them.

Due to the exclusive and private nature of this program, *WIN WIN WIN* is only available by contacting me directly and including information about your membership program or consulting business. If you think you have the right type of business for this program, email me and I will be happy to send you a copy of *WIN WIN WIN*.

60 Minute Shooks

For the individual who wants the fastest path to having a published shook with his or her name on it, I have a growing collection of shooks I have created and are available to be licensed by others.

60-Minute Shooks are already-written shooks on a range of topics, including marketing tips, how to sleep better tips, insurance tips, and more will be added over time. You only need about 60-minutes to personalize the content to you and your business!

Licensing a 60-Minute Shook is a fast and efficient way to instantly become a published author and differentiate yourself from your competition. 60-Minute Shooks are licensed on an annual basis, and you have the option of having an entire shook-centric marketing campaign built for you. If you are interested in more details about our licensable 60-Minute Shooks, visit BiteSizedBooks.com.

Ready to Get Started?

When you are ready to get started with any of my shook publishing programs, the very first step is a 15-minute Shook Strategy Session with me, so I can better understand your business and goals. Remember, every important and valuable journey starts with that first critical step. Schedule a session with me today and get started on the process of creating what I think is one of the smartest and most valuable marketing and business assets you can create—your very own short, helpful book!

CHAPTER 13

THE NEXT STEP

I f you've arrived on this page after reading this entire shook—thank you and congratulations. I hope I have gotten you excited about the potential of working together and publishing your own customer-attraction shook!

Imagine what it will feel like to hold and show your family your shook with your name on the cover as the author. Think about the satisfaction you'll get when a new customer tells you, "I read your book and had to meet you." Trust me, it's gratifying and makes the effort of creating your shook worthwhile.

My shook publishing programs are not inexpensive and are definitely not for everybody, but relative to the multitude of other ways you can invest your marketing dollars, my Main Street Author Programs are a bargain and will give you a hugely valuable business asset you will be able to leverage for years to come!

I am a firm believer you are uniquely qualified to be working with certain people—not everybody but people who "get" you and what you and your business stand for. I feel the same about my business and in order for us to see if we are a good fit, I have a simple and easy way to further explore this opportunity and it all starts with a 15-minute Shook Strategy Session between you and me. This will give us a chance to "meet" and see if working together makes sense. To schedule this call, here's what to do...

Step #1—Visit MainStreetAuthor.com.

Step #2—Review my publishing opportunities

Step #3—Click the Shook Strategy Session button and follow the prompts to schedule a call with me.

This one-on-one call with me will help me understand what you do and what your goals are. This call is all about helping you decide if working together to get your shook done is a good fit for both of us. It's a two-way interview to make sure we agree this is a good match.

I look forward to hearing from you, and more importantly, working together to turn you into a Main Street Author and help you create one of the most powerful and effective marketing assets you can create for your business—your very own shook.

Thank you!

ABOUT MIKE CAPUZZI

Mike is a publisher, author, consultant and coach for business owners looking to get to the next level in their business. Throughout his 25 years in marketing and 21 years as a consultant, Mike's innovative use of High Impact Marketing has consistently surpassed the expectations and outcomes of traditional marketing concepts and business strategies for his clients.

This expertise has led him to be a guest speaker on the stages of some of the world's most foremost experts on marketing, including Dan Kennedy, Bill Glazer, Rory Fatt, Ed Rush and Julie Steinbacher. To date, Mike has helped thousands of business owners create more profitable marketing.

Mike is the inventor of the wildly successful software product, CopyDoodles®. CopyDoodles are hand-drawn graphic files that enable anybody to literally drag and drop attention-grabbing enhancements to their offline and online marketing materials. Tens of thousands of business owners, marketers and copy-writers have benefited from the use of CopyDoodles.

In 2019, Mike launched Bite Sized Books, a new publishing venture founded on his proven formula for creating short, helpful books (known as shooks) for Main Street business owners. Shooks are ideal for local business owners who are looking to increase their level of authority, while also providing helpful information in bite sized books. Check out his Main Street Author Podcast at MikeCapuzzi.com.

When he's not focused on marketing or helping his clients, Mike is the proud father of two beautiful daughters, Caroline and Nicole. Caroline, who is attending Penn State University to study journalism, published her first shook, *Dog Joy,* in 2018. Dog Joy is a collection of dog rescue stories as told by the people who rescued them. She has donated all the profits from *Dog Joy* (over $5,000) to help support a number of the rescues featured in the shook.

Mike has been married to his amazing wife Becky for 23 years and counting. Becky is the invisible driving force behind everything Mike does to serve clients, including being the original handwriting artist for CopyDoodles.

To learn more about Mike's opportunities, visit MikeCapuzzi.com. If you're looking for a content-rich, unique speaker for your in-person or virtual event, contact Mike at friend@mikecapuzzi.com.

THE MAIN STREET AUTHOR PODCAST

The Main Street Author Podcast is an interview-style podcast with host Mike Capuzzi and local Main Street business owners who have successfully authored, published and leveraged a book in their business to differentiate themselves and attract more ideal customers, clients, patients or students.

Each episode is focused on book-authoring and book-centric marketing tactics and strategies that work for traditional local business owners. Even though you may have never heard of some of Mike's guests, you're sure to get several ideas and nuggets of wisdom that are proven to work in the real world of face-to-face business.

Check it out at MikeCapuzzi.com and if you think you would make a suitable guest on the Main Street Author Podcast, visit MikeCapuzzi.com/guest and connect with Mike.

"I appreciate your
feedback!"

A SMALL FAVOR

Thank you for reading *Main Street Author*! I am positive if you follow what I've written (and shared with the bonus training), you will be on your way to being a Main Street Author! When you do, please send me a copy of your shook so I can show it off!

I have a small, quick favor to ask. Would you mind taking a minute or two and leaving an honest review for this shook on Amazon? Reviews are the BEST way to help others purchase this shook, and I check all my reviews looking for helpful feedback. Visit:

MainStreetAuthor.com/review

If you have any questions or run into some challenges or if you would just like to tell me what you think about *Main Street Author*, shoot me an email at support@mainstreetauthor.com. I'd love to hear from you!

Don't Forget to Download Your Two Bonus Gifts!

Because you bought this shook, you get two valuable, *must-have* bonus gifts I created exclusively for readers of Main Street Author.

The first gift is a "lost chapter" on *The Power of Undivided Attention*, which I wrote after finalizing Main Street Author but want you to have.

The second gift is a special companion training, *How to Design & Print Your Shook,* I created just for readers of *Main Street Author.* This exclusive training, which complements this shook, goes into greater detail on how to design your cover and interior and how to print your shook. It gives you *must-have* insights you should know to get your shook done quickly and easily!

DOWNLOAD TODAY!

www.MainStreetAuthor.com/gifts

Made in the USA
Middletown, DE
28 December 2019